The Ineffable: Words Unspoken, Thoughts Unheard, Feelings Unknown

Joseph Foo

Presentation by *BookLeaf Publishing*

Web: www.bookleafpub.com

E-mail: info@bookleafpub.com

ISBN: 9789357443210

First edition 2023

To my mother who taught me that words are beautiful gifts and that poetry is the perfect wrapping.

PREFACE

I have been deliberating on how I should structure the poems and I finally decided to order them according to 9 specific themes that mirror my emotional journey through most experiences in life. These poems come from a range of inspirations, including friends, music, random walks and so on. They do not speak of a singular event but rather the general development of each episode in life. The poems are arranged as such:

1) An invitation into the enigmatic world of poetry (poems 1-2)

2) A humorous and carefree spirit as we see things for the first time (poems 3-4)

3) A vague and gradual realisation that life is not so simple (poems 5-6)

4) Careful thought reveals the depth of even the simplest experience (poems 7-8)

5) Choices are made as we soon realise that paths often diverge (poems 9-11)

6) Uncertainty and regrets will often cause us to doubt ourselves (poems 12-14)

7) Nevertheless, true kinship is our anchor as we brave the storm (poems 15-16)

8) Good things must come to an end and nostalgia sets in (poems 17-18)

9) As we lay the past to rest, we look to the future with hope (poems 19-21)

It might seem paradoxical to write about the ineffable sublimity of life, considering how rich, complex and bizarre life can be. However, what I have attempted here is not to reify the infinite permutations of life into words. Instead, I hope that through these poems, we can embark on a journey of retrospection and self-discovery, filling in tiny pieces in the unsolvable puzzle of our lives, appreciating where we came from and where we want to go, even if we don't have and can't have all the answers to life.

The Poetic Durian

If you prod my spiky skin
  Trying to reach the flesh within,
I will enjoy watching you bleed
  A pinprick, red as a saga seed.

But fear me not, though I seem forbidden,
  Tempting as the Apple in the Garden of Eden.
For I shall unveil your hidden desire,
  To burn your ignorance, in a rain of fire.

So delve into me and go bananas,
  For I am like water in the tropical savannas,
Simple and unassuming, as a watermelon green,
  But filled with crimson sweetness, flowing
from my skin.

A Piano's Dream

Suspended by silver wings
on a thread, our dreams on a feather,
floats gently through the sky and
lands itself on a note.
Hope, love and peace
once broken by accord -
The root - your door,
Hold to the sound,
go through to a
world beyond
A world of dreams
Monde de rêves
Sparkling, shiny, shimmers.
Glistening, giddy, glitters...
You must go on,
They say third time's the
charm, let not fear your heart
disarm, for highs and lows are
but a sum, of who we eventually
were meant to
become...
Come now, not all is lost
We must endure,
no matter the cost.
Fortune favours the bold

that's what you were told, so
let me give you a gift -
here you are, a perfect fifth.
So come, let your dreams toward me float,
I'll carry your burden, I'll carry your load.
For what was once broken by accord,
Shall now live in me, together, as
one chord.

The Po(or)tatoes

I am a royal potato whose shape is a perfect
oval,
My fame is so widespread that everyone knows
me from the stars to Mars.
This uncontrollable charm I exude is so novel,
that even the queens and kings before me grovel.

Even though this tale may not seem real,
I would still appreciate if you would go to my
palace just to say hello.

These days, times have been hard, for the
invincible McDonalds has
been winning countless victories.
My young comrades from the north have been
skinned and stripped to pieces.
My amazing xylophone that would make the
zealous moon jealous has been
burnt in the fire and trampled in the mire.

We must push for the rights of potatoes
Just like the tomatoes
Whose fire and concept of equality
Has driven hungry humans to see reality.
If it was them in the frying pan,

Would it still excite them to ignite
The fire that burns so painfully bright?

I'm Hungry

While you are learning about a bandage,
I'm somewhere eating a sandwich.
Sigh, my big stomach feels guilty.

While you rush of somewhere to save a life,
I'll probably be destroying a beef steak with a
knife.
Ah, I'm so hungry.

What kind of first aid kit is this? You may yell -
Meanwhile, I'm looking for what food they sell.
There's the difference, oh well.

Many lives you positively touch,
Even when no one expects much.
So may your kindness burn brightly,
While my stomach growls on…slightly.

In Between

An orange haze, shapeless birds in the sky -
Sea foams wash against an empty shore.
Breathe in, feel the wind and soar...
Step into the light, let your dreams and reality
In this mystical realm collide
Feel your breath hang between the air
Like a wisp of smoke that blinds your stare
The fire burns brighter, the water rise higher
breathless breathless a spiral of despair

Savour the sights

In the evening sky, when hangs
like a curtain an orange curtain,
through clouds unseen, the sun
its glories bring.
We often call it a sunset,
yet it's the simple clouds that bear
this phenomenon we gloriously sing.
When through vales and valleys,
o'er mountains and streams we tread,
how often we gaze at the majestic marvels,
but simple flowers forget to savour?
Perhaps it's hard to imagine what I
speak off, but do you feel the veil coming off
as you savour tasteless joy and
see the sightless beauty,
as you begin through life's long journey?

Still waters run deep

You may not believe in sentiments
Weak to you it may seem
Like useless condiments
In a dish overflowing with flavour.

Yet, I'll still tell you of my gratitude,
For your presence in my life,
Never overbearing, but always there.
In you I've confided, my thoughts
and feelings to share.
You had no obligations,
Still you always care.

Your mind is like a whirlwind of dust,
It churns and burns anyone who dares draw near.
For the complexities of who you are,
Would make any lesser man shudder in fear.

Good were the days of messing around,
From philosophy to business to religion,
To others our discourse might make them drown,
But boy were those times amazing.

The waves of time can erode the memories of
sand,

But I believe ours is built firmly with a bond,
One that even my words cannot fully
comprehend,
So here's to a friendship that the test of time will
stand!

Intellectual Noodles

As a bowl of noodles cannot my stomach fill,
So does my infant mind hunger still.
Can you the thirst for knowledge feel?
It's greater than the Monday recess queue.

Our conversations have largely
Left me hanging on thoughts
That were never there,
Opening doors in perception
That I didn't know were locked
From the inside.

If

If the sun were to forever shine...
And were we to bath in its eternal light,
One day we would look up in cynical wonder,
Asking if the nightless days were actually a
plight.

If laughter filled our every day...
And to sadness and despair we refuse to fall,
What would the meaning of life be,
But that of a mindless thrall?

In these fleeting moments of life,
We race for the horizons of tomorrow,
Refusing to look back at yesterday's strife -
Every second, every minute, from eternity we
borrow.
Running from death's cold scythe
Into a world free of sorrow.

But. I refuse to live a life of serenity,
Drowning in a dream of reality.
You taught me how to see beyond this earth
Ignite a spark, my creativity to birth.
A Word of thanks, a Paean of praise
Insufficient they are, my thanks to raise -

So let us face forward
and let us seize the day.

Should I...

Should I go right? Where nothing is left.
A barren land, a thirsty sea.
Or should I go left? Where nothing is right.
A world of hate, a chasm of love.
Empty buildings, vacant eyes,
They stare at hope
Despair gazes back
Nothing breathes, all is still.
Chaos ensues, a riot of colours.
The drunk are a haze.
Let your lust run ablaze
All is good, don't dampen the mood.
Will you get busy living?
In a world full of sinning?
Or will you get busy dying?
In a world not worth trying?

It's not a small world

15

The world is bigger than you and me,
Possibilities wider than the sky and sea.
Some men make it up the mountain peak,
Some men dive to the depths of oceans deep.
And some still, snuggle in a cafe for a coffee sip.

We're all one in this floating bubble.
Ages later we'll be under rubble…
Think not of what the future could be,
For it is a possibility we might not see.
Just enjoy the present while we're free
Cause the world is much bigger than you and
me.

Shadows of Intent

A shooting star, a ray of light,
A streak of hope, a glorious flight.
Could it be so without darkness dim?
Illuminate the love between you and him?

We crawl on fours through the tunnel tight,
Hoping for Ithaca - the end in sight.
Yet, can one with full assurance say,
Our hearts be renewed with the dawn of day?

For each tragedy you will befall,
Your heart a darkness shall surely call.
The deep recess of human thought,
Through pain and suffering to the light now
brought.

Embrace the darkness that's deep within,
But purge the evil and be free of sin.

Gilgamesh

Mid the stormy seas and wailing breeze,
And rocks caressed by a single wave,
A moment of grief shall time now freeze,
The King of Heroes who can he save?

Standing above the towers tall,
He sits enthroned with jewels bright,
Yet on his knees he must now fall,
For mortality shall now vanquish his pride.

Of gods and myths he always swore,
To rid the world - but like Odysseus's men,
Bewitched by the charming Circe's call,
From glory to ashes to grains of sand.

Echoes

Great kings of old
In death all equal.
Their hands they fold
Stained with much evil.

Fame above, their victories sound,
Under the earth, the echoes drown.

You

How wonderful life has been
  Another amazing friend I have seen
   The waves of time shall forever sing
    How these blissful days shall repeatedly ring
     A melodious symphony, an unbroken string
      Were I to be granted one wish upon a fairy's wing
       All I would ask is for you to know, just how much I'm thankful for
        You

Fade: (Out) Memories - (In) Friendship

Can you remember the start of a dream?
The thoughts that flow in an endless stream?
     I cannot for that's how it is -
Or at least so it would seem.

Do you remember each word we've spoken?
Each time the boredom of going home was
broken?
     I cannot; for each day passes in a blink -
Or perhaps not until I from my sleep have
woken.

I cannot recall the journeys of each day
remember,
the countless days from January to December.
I've felt some of your personal pain,
And hope I will, that your trust in me, will still
remain.

For though I cannot describe the journey of our
friendship,
Do I really need to jot down each moment?
Those days have been like stars in the twilight,

that live on to a new dawn, shining equally
bright.

Flames of Passion, Embers of Love

A fire roars,
It brightly burns.
A summer falls,
For life we yearn.

Each day is a maze,
We walk in a daze.
A flicker of hope,
We must be brave.

Through cold nights,
A warmth from within
Though impossibly thin,
From despair makes light.

As sure as the days will roll,
My gratitude you must know.
That like a fire in my life,
You can burn through snow.
Buried in the past
I do not know how this will end...
perhaps, I should not even lift my pen -
A ghost you were in the year before
Nothing about you did I adore.

What could have happened then?
descend did I, into sinking sand?
I never knew about you
Yet here I am.

Speaking of days buried in the past
In my mind, in vain, they were left to rust.
Your smile was bright. Your soul a light.
The piano was your voice, a voice so bright…
My words are flowing out, but here they must
- end -
For these memories, are buried in the past.

Unrequited

Is happiness nothing but a shimmering star?
That lights the moment but fades from afar?

Is friendship perhaps, like a flourishing flower?
Which blossoms in summer but yields to
winter's power?

I cannot tell for a cloud of doubt has covered me
whole,
The sweeter days trampled under the frosty
white snow.

Is it possible for the heart to feel
The feeling of nothing
and our words to speak…
The meaning of something
so far beyond our comprehension;
Paralysing us. In apprehension?

Time will flow, I'll wait for summer's snow.
On our way we must go for we cannot slow.
Should I still long, still hope, still wait,
For a star that might never sparkle…

Each step I take, each moment I wake…

Can you promise that these memories you'll
take?
Hold them tight. Don't let them break.

Laughter is the best medicine

Happy happy the morning goes,
Weary weary the noontime grows.
By mid day, my brain juice is dry…

But there sits in front of me a cauldron
Of absolute delight,
Whose smile and laughter
Can make the dull days bright.

So smile and laugh
For your warmth and
Liveliness is like the sun,
Heralding a light that breaks
Through life's every plight.

The Promised Land

Through the summer blaze,
Our souls be weary filled
We lift our heads, up to gaze -
How long more must the lands be tilled?

When autumn comes and the leaves descend,
A defiant waltz of life in its final breath.
The last chorus of the sparrows ascend,
Has Hope too for fairer plains left?

So when the snow begins to fall,
In whispers and showers like a coat of fur.
Shall we also answer the wakeless dreams that
call...
Or is there hope beyond the drop of myrrh?

For Christ did suffer too, he bled and he died.
For you and me, our sorrows are but a shadow.
Let the warmth of spring dry the tears that were
cried,
And walk joyfully onwards to that heavenly
meadow.

Press On!

28

On clouds of dust, our feet have trod.
We race towards the morrow, that's out of reach.
The battles we've won and fought
And those from which we must retreat.

They make our life, a book with pages filled
Our future. A mystery. We must be thrilled!
Let's press on towards the setting sun
We'll remember the days of endless fun
And meet again, when all's said and done!